IN RETROSPECT

Iona Matheson

KEELHALLA PUBLICATIONS, ISLE OF RAASAY
INVERNESS-SHIRE

Printed by Bookmag, Henderson Road, Inverness

PREFACE

"The prismatic beauty of Iona Matheson's poetry makes each reading a further, new experience. Her images are created with bold confidence, and always behind them, related, is the bleak splendour of Wester Ross."

Jackson Webb

ACKNOWLEDGEMENTS

With grateful thanks, to Murdo for his illustrations, to Julie, for her Celtic Design, and to my family and friends for their support and encouragement

TO
MY FAMILY

WHAT AM I TO WRITE?

What am I to write for you?
Blank page,
White emptiness,
Broken words are not enough
Nor spluttered ink spat out in ignorance,
Contemptuous of its desire to mark
And maim,
Indulges so at first,
And then again.
But No
I will not take to mediocre ways,
Nor overplay the passion song in muse,
For the heart well tuned
Needs not the head
To pump its life,
And the arteries awakened to the rhythm,
Subtle rhythm,
Should suffice.

LAND OF THE SMALL RAIN

The Day of the 'Great Maclean' has gone,
The progress parasite is eating up the ancient soul
And soon there will be nothing left
Except, maybe
The 'Blue Cuillin' and the small rain
Ah! the small rain,
Its music sings in the very marrow of the Celtic bone
There is no malice within that white vein,
And to them
Of the empty weakling shells
I reserve my pity.

The Kindred smile
I knew it well
But seldom does it come forth now,
Its utterance is liken to the splutter of the dying candle flame
And the heart of her pain cries out to be rekindled,
For she knows
That the 'Bog Myrtle' will give up her fragrance
For a better eternity,
And she leaves
No forwarding address.

WHISTLE DOWN THE WIND.

Enveloped in the mist of you,
Yet able to find my way
And clear sighted.

Drowned in the darkling of your gaze,
Yet anchored to my faith
And sweetly safe.

Remembered are the pains of wistful longing,
And all your oblivion of these little miseries
Is not despised,
Your love has been elsewhere,
And jealousy has gone, untried.

Trusted to you
Are all of poetry's thoughts,
The kind that girlish fancy has not bought,
And though in sense this is a tragic state,
Just whistle down the wind,
I'll wait.

THE JESTERS MASK

Guard those childish fantasies
That make you trust whole heartedly,
Make haste to thought
Before that perilous tongue
Has mocked your inner meaning,
And watch too, those actions
Like dancers, slipping unaware
From the rhythm of understanding,
Few will comprehend
The true fashion of your nature,
And to wear the 'Jesters' mask
That he might tears protect,
Is a risk,
For all can see that,
But who, shall see through it?

PHILOSOPHY

To live
Is to love . . .

To love
Is to give . . .

To give
Is to take,
And to regive
Again.

CELT

Honesty
in all its complexity
Truth
in all its deceptiveness
Content
in the awakening
of the soul
Your eyes
are full of feeling
and a solitude
is born there
Torn
'twixt life and living
pain plays
a plaintive air
And though
thy honest heart
has voice
'Tis yours to ask
and yours by choice
For truth is there
dear friend be swift
Content
is as the changeling
mist . . .

Be lifted
into my eyes hunger
Feast with me
in the beauty
of a song
become the morning
of the Clarsach
give rise
to Celtic throng
For we
still young
yet ages passed
Find youth
through death
And free
at last.

FOR KAY MATHESON

WOMAN OF THE SEA

To the men of the sea
Who sail with the wind
And are free,
To the Land that has borne them
And the seed that has torn them
From me,
For I gave it willing, without grieving,
To the sons of my soul,
Who in seeking the truth of existence
Have quenched the starvation in me,
For I, am but woman,
And all, 'tis all I shall be.

FOR DUNCAN

AMBASSADORS FROM THE DEEP

ORCA
You have come to us,
From the midnight
Of the deep.

ORCA
You have awakened us,
From a death like arrogance
Of sleep.

ORCA
You have brought us
From the fear of the unknown,

GREAT DOLPHIN
Of the emerald sky,
Gently, take us home.

ORCA
You have given birth
In the captivity of trust

ORCA
You shall guide us there,
As the earth's song says you must.

AMBASSADORS
From one whose love
Is greater than our greed,

ORCA
You have come to us,
From the midnight
Of the deep.

MAN OF THE SEA

For the woman I see
Who stands by the rock,
And the tree,
Who put meaning and measure and might
Into all things
For me,
Who taught songs of the earth
And showed me the places of light,
Who then put the 'Orb' in my hand,
And bade me the Final Goodnight.
.   .   .   .

No man ever born
Could make courage to riseth
Like She,
This spirit that dwells
And excels,
And is living, through me.

DRIFT NOT . . .

Drift not with dreams
But take them
In their fullest flood,
And pledge your soul to honesty,

Grasp the moment
Steal the sigh,
And make it seem
To laugh, or cry.

Drift not with Barley's heady dew,
But take the wine
In measured glass,
And kiss the spirits melody,

Timbre the moment,
Caress the sigh,
And touch the song
To fill the eye.

FOR DONNIE MACLENNAN

THE THIRD RIGHT ...

The silver shroud
Transparent into birth . . .

The white shroud
Transparent unto death . . .

And further,
That thou mayest see,

The golden shroud
Which encompass the sun,

And deep, into the heart
Of the unknown . . .

ONLY THE BLIND

Only the blind can see
Into the depths of light,
That dark shadow
Awakening.

Only the blind can hear
Beyond the horizon
Of that brilliant sound,
Partaking.

Only the blind can touch
Feeling above measure,
That serenity in grace,
Relating.

FOR JULIE

THE REVELATION

What is this mystery?
This agonizing passion in the breast
Of those, who dream.
Whose thoughts when born cause pain
But will not be denied,
Whose inner search for truth
Lies dormant for a time,
And then ascends,
Is beckoned by the tide.

What is this light?
This ever glowing passion in the eyes
Of those, who know.
Whose false piety is cast away
Whose eyes have lost that vacant stare,
And where once the teardrop
Burned the darkened socket,
With one swift glance
One silken beam of sunlight
From those transcendant pools,
Would cause the very rock
Of Acheron's tomb
To stir.

And then as if from 'Babylon Heights'
A voice transcends,
A vision echoes
Ethereal, ecstasy sublime,
Its tranquil shadow radiant
In robes of scarlet dawn,
Seems gently to caress this single soul,
And cast it softly
Upon the shores,
Of that celestial paradise
Beyond all earthly bondage.

NAKED, INTO THE SUN

What is it like to be you?
I nearly wonder,
Sparkling, gleaming child,
Well nourished little body,
Covered in such fine linen.
If I were so beautiful,
I should fly!
Naked, into the sun,
Clothed only in my gratitude
Laughing and dancing.
.   .   .   .

Ah, but your eyes,
They are such childish little eyes,
Mine, are full of feeling,
The soul of Christ is in my eye,
And my hungry tears
Is his heart,
Bleeding.

POUR LE CHIEN.

You are seeming to a melody
That lingers,
Leaving a pain more generous
Than was intent,
And your eyes compassion
Remembered,
Shall sweeten the slumber,
In a cold grave.

EPITAPH TO THE 'BATTERY HEN'.

PLUCK THE WISH-BONE ...

Pluck the wish-bone
From the dead bird
Forget the bird, 'tis easy,
What care you for her agony?

She could not fly,
Nor play a pretty songstress chord
For memory to consume,
But with the wish-bone you will mock
Her silent, lifeless tune.

And then in 'Pagan Ritual'
The bone is broke, the spell is cast,
Think you, there is mercy in her marrow
To grant such pathetic whims, illusions,
And none so pitiful
As the one you created of her,

That she had no agony ...

DANCE OF THE BLESSED SPIRITS.

THEIRS
Is the true burning
Of existence,
The never ending flight.

THEIRS
Is the sanctuary
Of newly born unity,
Continual peace.

THEIRS
Is freedoms passion
Blessed,
Musical fluency.

RUTH CLARE.

Ruth Clare
Spoke,
And sighed,
A simple sigh,
She was lost
And so was I.

Then trees shadowed the world beyond,
Dreams floated by,
Voices, images, and satire conversationalists
Focused their confusion
On the last summer Swan,
She sang.

Confusion was static,
And Magicians fell to foolish ways,
"We will carry the coffin" they jeered.
"Idiots of idolatry" cried the Owl
"She will not die,
She is giving birth to a new world".

RUTH CLARE IN GREEN

When lifes dream
Soakes up what is not there
And ceases to be real,
'Ruth Clare'
Will come
And beckon you
To prayer,
Sister of the forest
Elphin Queen,
Myth she be
Or legend
Adorned in green.
Sister of the wind,
Fairy of the twilight dew,
She will hear
While all the rest
Turn frigid,
Blue.
So come now
From your medieval casks,
Live not in future
Nor in presents past,
But grasp the trinity
In momentary form,
As like e'er lasting green
Which compliments the thorn.

FROM THE TRYSTING PLACE.

They appeared
In the mist
Of each others eye,

A violet shadow
Enveloped the green canopy
Where they slumbered,

Awakened in unison
By the same ghost's breath,
And the one thought.

TO . . .

To every day its hour,
To every moment its magic spell,
To every sorrow its comfort,
To every love its private hell.
To every merriment its mirth,
To every move its meaning,
To every hope its hopefulness,
To every truth its triumph.

To 'Don Mclean' who came
And brought his song,
To long lost friends who left,
And 'Lady Memory' has claimed,
To misty mornings born of sunrise born
Of sunset echoed sighs from ancient days,
To masquerades of colour which transform
And to all their different shades.

To the music of the earth
That speaks in silver tones,
To those who hear
And rise to her calling,
To the sacred dance
That sprung from dust and toil,
To those who perform
And worship in its dawning.

To every soul, the will, to be,
To every mind, the eye, to see,
For those who do
And those who don't
And those who can't see what they want,
Have pity on the blind,
For they're not free

To be . . .

RINGS AROUND THE POOL.

And still the sea
At Camusfearna,
Rings around the pool,
All of nature echoes here
For him
Who's gone, too soon.

And calm the sea
In Sandaig's wood,
Mijbil's song resounds,
All earth's pleasures captured here
By him,
Whom pain unbound.

And peaceful the sea
By Edal's grave,
The Rowan Knights do sleep,
And kinder the thoughts that lingered here,
Of him,
That we shall keep.

IN MEMORY OF GAVIN MAXWELL

ISLAND AWAKENING.

The land is whispering us back,
Far back, like a distant echo
From a deep slumber,
She is stirring,
And the song of the Seal
Is heard at Castle.
The land is calling us,
Calling us back to herself,
Light giving, and tender,
Inspiring old dreams to rebirth
She is awakening,
And the Otter's laughter plays
On the shore at Fearns.

The land is willing us,
Haunting our conscience
To return
And find the home of selfless enterprise,
Become the energy of Hallaig's rock,
She is moving,
And the Skylark sings
Over Glam.

FOR SHONA MACLEAN

THE POPPY.

Whose soul was that I bought today,
Or was it just a fantasy
Of time,
Unlimited, unjust.
O' glorious figures in swaddling clothes
Of grey decay,
Whose speechless eyes,
But know the song of truth so well,
For His names sake
And theirs,
The dumb secret, awake within
The mocking head, reflecting all.

How sweet the pain of death to those
Of whom lifes water drained,
All hope sunk deep in 'Blighty' lads
Where only men doth weep,
And mercies droplets falling fast
Like rain upon the soul,
Leave bitter sweet, the memory,
Unborn, but dead, and gone.
. . . . . .
Anguish burns within the innocence
Of thought,
And we, can only think.

M. Nicolson

THE YOUNG MAN WITH THE WOODEN LEG

He came into my life
For a brief moment only,
We sat together
And watched 'Edith Piaf'
Singing.
He said that he liked her,
It was the only thing he said,
And I understood why.
She had been born in the street,
He, had just come from it.
She was strong, and a fighter,
She had left it,
He was not
And had been swept into the flood.
He had a wooden leg, you see,
And as she kept on regretting nothing
He felt nothing,
But bitterness,
And I wanted to comfort,
Like a sickly mother
Over a stillborn child.

THE HIDEOUS.

Mastery over sea and sky
Master of whether to live or die
They can pluck the foetus from the womb
And prolong the longing for the tomb.

Mastery over earth and air
Master of whatever species to spare
They can all play 'God' and decide at will
Whom and what they're going to kill.

Mastery over woman and child
Master of power's lust, gone wild
They can rape and mutilate treasures of earth
And escape the Law, for what it's worth.

Mastery over space and time
Master of whether the light should shine
They can 'Blast' us all to 'Kingdom Come'
And turn to smile on the work they've done.

But Who is Master of the Man?
For long since now, his pace outran,
He has outgrown himself, by far,
Outraged the balance of this star.
. . . .
Watch, how the winds and seasons change,
And wait on Nature's cold revenge.

THE HIDEOUS, CONDEMNED.

The ugly concept of their guilt
On unassuming innocence
Renders in them
An
Anguished cry
A plea
From their abandonment
They stood together in my mind
As timeless time passed by.

REQUIEM
FOR JULIA HASTINGS MACLEOD.

And out of the green dusk
She came to me,
In a potent breeze
Unashamed, complete.

And out of the green dusk
She shaded me,
In all the magic of death,
So innocent and sweet.

And in her gaze
A tiger slumbers there,
A tenderness of wisdom
In an all consuming prayer.

Child of the morning,
Ghost, by the midnight hour,
Cut down in the wake of your dawning,
What Hellish hand was there?

A mystery of justice?
Tell me the Gods that care
Where are the reasons, the answers,
And why does she seem so fair
Why does she have a childish glance,
But a woman's restless Air?

Iona

'EMILY'

I dreamt I saw the crags
From which your soul
Was carved,
And from their depths
A hungry shadow watched,
But did not stare.

Your body is the moss and lichen
There,
Pressed gentle as a child
On a mothers breast
Of clay.

Your breath is of that savage hush
Called wind,
Whispering, beckoning,
And howling to life the moorland,
Most beloved, and haunted place.

Your spirit is the moon's shadow
Within the darkened crag,
Hungry for solitude
Yet ever watching,
Always there,
And shining.

CATRIONA'S SONG FOR OLIVER.

In the morn
When all is new,
And Autumns chilly frost.

In the morn
When all is dew,
And copper leaves are tossed.

Gift to you fair natures child
The wings of freedom glossed,
Appearing in a golden cloud
And envied by the Gods.

Bring to life primeval light
And let my senses boast,
Their courage
Through your high desire,
You are in my soul,
Always be my ghost
Always be my ghost.

FOR PIPPY

SEANNACHIES

To have listened with them
In a twilight shade,
Amidst the forest's darkened glade,
To have silence piled around my feet
And their thoughts, like leaves,
To cover me.

To have spoken with them
In a timeless room,
From within the Warrior's ageless tomb,
To die in the ruins of this night
And their words, like wounds,
To waken me.

To have knelt with them
In a valley green,
Where earthbound souls are rarely seen,
To battle with solitude all my days
And their prayers, like swords,
To strike me.